THE USBORNE
ART
Sticker Book

Sarah Courtauld and Kate Davies

Illustrated by Holly Surplice

Designed by Nicola Butler   Edited by Rosie Dickins   Consultant: Kathy Adler

American Editor: Carrie Armstrong

CONTENTS

Published in association with
National Gallery Company Limited

ANIMALS

You can find lots of animals in paintings – and some unusual
or important animals get a whole painting to themselves...

This painting is detailed and vivid, but Rousseau never went anywhere near a jungle. He had to go to the zoo to draw this tiger.

The tiger has a surprised look on his face, as he's just spotted some explorers.

Rousseau said the tiger was about to pounce on the explorers, but he didn't show them in the painting .

Surprised!
1891
Henri Rousseau

Kittens often appear in paintings as symbols of childhood, as they're innocent and playful – but wild at the same time.

A group of people in carnival masks have gathered to look at a famous rhino, named Clara. They would never have seen a rhino before.

The rhino's owner is holding up its horn, which has been chopped off.

A Girl with a Kitten
1745
Probably by
Jean-Baptiste Perronneau

Exhibition of a Rhinoceros at Venice
About 1751
Pietro Longhi

The Vision of Saint Eustace
1438–42
Pisanello

This is a painting of a religious vision that Saint Eustace had while he was hunting. He suddenly saw Jesus in the antlers of a deer. Pisanello used the story as an excuse to show lots of different animals.

a hare

dogs

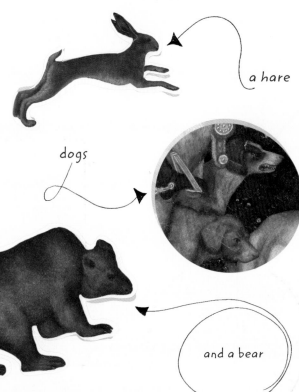

and a bear

A Lady with a Squirrel and a Starling
About 1526–8
Hans Holbein the Younger

Some people did actually have pet squirrels in the 16th century, but Holbein probably included one in this painting because the lady's family had a squirrel in their coat of arms.

Whistlejacket was a star racehorse of his day. Stubbs painted this portrait for his proud owner.

In real life, the painting is almost the size of a real horse, which shows how important Whistlejacket was. Portraits this big usually showed kings.

Whistlejacket
About 1762
George Stubbs

FABULOUS FASHION

In the past, nearly everyone wore their finest clothes
to have their portraits painted, so they'd look their best.
But sometimes, they dressed up as characters they admired.

Mr. and Mrs. Andrews wouldn't really have worn such fine clothes to go shooting, but they wanted to show off their huge country estate and their expensive outfits in the same painting. However, they didn't want to sit outside for hours and hours, so Gainsborough used wooden models dressed up in their clothes, and painted in their faces afterward.

Gainsborough didn't always draw his landscapes from life. He made little models, using lumps of coal for rocks, and broccoli for trees.

Mr. and Mrs. Andrews
About 1750
Thomas Gainsborough

The women and children in bonnets are dressed in the latest fashions of late 19th-century Paris. But the woman carrying the basket wears the plain street clothes of a working woman. She was originally wearing a frilly bonnet, too, but Renoir repainted her several years after he'd finished the painting.

This x-ray shows what she used to look like.

Portrait of a Young Man
About 1540–5
Moretto da Brescia

The Umbrellas
1881–6
Pierre-Auguste Renoir

This nobleman is dressed in luxurious furs, to show how rich he is. But even though he's wealthy, he doesn't look happy. There's some writing on his hat, which reads: "Alas, I desire too much."

4

Doña Isabel de Porcel
Before 1805
Francisco de Goya

This stylish Spanish lady is dressed up in the style of a flamenco dancer. Traditional outfits like these became very fashionable in 19th-century Spain. Women wore them to show how patriotic they were.

Rembrandt painted this portrait of his wife Saskia a year after their wedding. She is dressed up as Flora, goddess of Spring.

Saskia van Uylenburgh as Flora
1635
Rembrandt van Rijn

Ingres spent seven years trying to get Madame Moitessier's dress absolutely right. But one afternoon he started again and painted it all in one sitting.

Ingres wanted to show off her profile too, so he painted it reflected in the mirror. He had to cheat to do this, because the angle of the mirror means it would really have reflected the back of her head.

Madame Moitessier
1856
Jean-Auguste-Dominique Ingres

Portrait of a Lady
Probably 1465
Alesso Baldovinetti

The bold pattern on this woman's sleeve is probably her family emblem. Her headdress shows off her high forehead, which was fashionable at the time. Women even plucked out their hair to make their foreheads higher.

5

CHILDREN

In the past, some artists painted children to look just like little adults. But later on they began to show them playing and having fun, far away from the adult world.

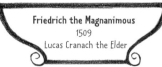

Friedrich the Magnanimous
1509
Lucas Cranach the Elder

This portrait was painted when Friedrich was only six years old. His father was the ruler of Saxony, in Germany, so he is painted to look intelligent and serious, like a future king.

These boys are having fun blowing bubbles, but there's a serious message to this painting. The artist has added the bubbles as a symbol of how short life is.

Two Boys blowing Bubbles
About 1670
Caspar Netscher

The Graham Children
1742
William Hogarth

This looks like a happy family, but by the time the portrait was finished, the baby on the left had died.

Hogarth included symbols of time passing in this painting. There's a clock in the top left corner, and on top of it stands a figure holding a scythe, a symbol of death. The cat looks as if it wants to eat the bird, and there's also a dying flower at the baby's feet.

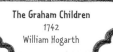

Some children had to work to earn a living. The girl on the right is working as a teacher, even though she's still a child herself.

This picture contrasts good behavior with bad behavior. The girl is learning to read, but the boy has turned his back on his lessons to play with a pet dog.

The Young Schoolmistress
Probably 1735-6
Jean-Siméon Chardin

This is a painting of three young children, but they are dressed in adult clothes and the way they're standing makes them look serious and grown-up.

A Lady teaching a Child to read, and a Child playing with a Dog
Probably 1670s
Caspar Netscher

The Balbi Children
About 1625-7
Anthony van Dyck

Gainsborough painted his two daughters chasing a butterfly on a summer's day. It was one of the first paintings to show children just being children.

The Painter's Daughters chasing a Butterfly
Probably 1756
Thomas Gainsborough

7

NATURE

Artists painted nature in lots of different ways.
Some artists used their surroundings to create atmospheric landscapes.
Others made arrangements of fruit and flowers, known as still lifes.

Van Gogh used swirls of bright colors in this painting,
to make it look as though wind is blowing the clouds
across the sky, ruffling the wheat and cypress trees.

A Wheatfield, with Cypresses
1889
Vincent van Gogh

Long Grass with Butterflies
1890
Vincent van Gogh

Even when he was just painting grass,
Van Gogh used thick, energetic brush
strokes to make it come alive. He created
the butterflies with just a few dabs of paint.

This still life looks very lifelike, but it's completely made-up.
Van Os took two years to paint it, because the different flowers
weren't all in bloom at the same time. It's also unlikely that
the pineapple could really have balanced on top.

Van Os included several animals and insects
in the painting, along with a bird's nest.

A mouse nibbling
on a walnut

Fruit and Flowers in a Terracotta Vase
1777-8
Jan van Os

A dragonfly
hovering near
the flowers

Van Rysselberghe made this calm coastal scene out of thousands of tiny dots. Close up, the dots form swirling, dancing patterns, like moonlight shimmering on water.

Coastal Scene
1892
Théo van Rysselberghe

The rows of tall trees and the long straight road encourage you to look into the distance, giving this painting a feeling of depth.

The Avenue at Middelharnis
1689
Meindert Hobbema

The Hay Wain
1821
John Constable

This is a painting of Suffolk, where Constable grew up. It's a hazy, nostalgic picture of a perfect summer's day — but he actually painted it from sketches in a studio in London, in the middle of winter.

This seascape shows a shipwrecked boat being tossed by the waves, while survivors scramble up the shore. Vernet makes the scene more dramatic by contrasting the darkness of the sea with the sunlight breaking through the clouds, far away.

This man and his dog are running for safety.

A Shipwreck in Stormy Seas
1773
Claude-Joseph Vernet

TOWNS AND CITIES

Many artists lived in towns and cities and wanted to paint cityscapes full of things going on, rather than peaceful scenes of nature.

Canaletto was famous for painting detailed views of Venice. This painting shows a gondola race at carnival time. Some of the people are wearing traditional carnival costumes.

Gondolas are narrow boats that are rowed with one long oar.

A Regatta on the Grand Canal
About 1740
Canaletto

Monet painted the Houses of Parliament several times, in different weather. Here he used soft, hazy colors to make the Houses of Parliament look ghostly on a misty morning and added dashes of dark paint for the rippling water.

The Boulevard Montmartre at Night
1897
Camille Pissarro

The Thames below Westminster
About 1871
Claude-Oscar Monet

Pissarro painted this from the window of his apartment in Paris. He drew the same view at different times of day. In this nighttime scene, he captured the shimmering reflections of streetlights on the wet, dark street.

Monet persuaded the train drivers at a Paris station to let out extra steam just for this painting. There's a roof over the station, but the puffs of steam look like clouds in the sky.

Pieter de Hooch painted many scenes of everyday life in Delft, the Dutch town where he lived. The plaque over the doorway still exists today. The broom and the neat flowerbed show that this was a well-run household.

The Courtyard of a House in Delft
1658
Pieter de Hooch

The Gare St-Lazare
1877
Claude-Oscar Monet

Avercamp was famous for painting bustling pictures of busy snowy scenes. The castle shown here is imaginary, but the painting is full of lifelike details.

A couple dressed in fine clothes

Two people slipping over on the ice

A Winter Scene with Skaters near a Castle
About 1608-9
Hendrick Avercamp

LIGHT

Artists use light and shadow to highlight the most important parts of their paintings and to make them look dramatic. Some artists also use light as a symbol of hope or goodness.

The old scientist is conducting an experiment on a bird to see whether it needs air to breathe. He's removing the air from the glass jar that the bird is in, and the bird is gasping for breath. Wright is using light to show us the most important part of the painting: the different reactions of all the people watching.

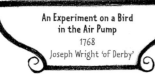

An Experiment on a Bird in the Air Pump
1768
Joseph Wright 'of Derby'

The scientist is looking at us, to see what we think.

This man looks serious, as though he's thinking about how fragile life is.

These girls are afraid the bird might die.

Monet wanted to capture the way sunlight reflected on water in his lily pond. He often worked on several paintings at the same time, running from one to the other, because he wanted to see how light changed during the day.

Water-Lilies
After 1916
Claude-Oscar Monet

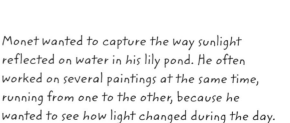

In many old religious paintings, light is a symbol of holiness. The Bible tells the story of King Belshazzar, who was at a feast when bright letters appeared on the wall in front of him, spelling out a warning from God. Belshazzar had been drinking from a stolen sacred cup. The writing on the wall reads: "Your days are numbered." That very night, Belshazzar was killed.

Belshazzar's Feast
About 1636–8
Rembrandt van Rijn

In this painting of the nativity, the baby Jesus lights up the whole scene. The angel above him also shines brightly in the darkness.

The Nativity at Night
About 1490
Geertgen tot Sint Jans

A young woman is standing next to a virginal, a musical instrument a bit like a piano, in the corner of a sunny room. Vermeer paints every detail of light and shade. The soft, delicate light gives the scene a calm, peaceful atmosphere.

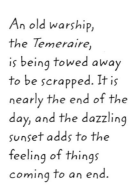

An old warship, the *Temeraire*, is being towed away to be scrapped. It is nearly the end of the day, and the dazzling sunset adds to the feeling of things coming to an end.

A Young Woman standing at a Virginal
About 1670–2
Johannes Vermeer

The Fighting Temeraire
1839
J.M.W.Turner

Turner often painted outdoors so he could get a good look at the effects of light and weather. He even claimed he once tied himself to a ship's mast in a storm to paint the ocean raging around him.

COLOR

Bold splashes of color do more than brighten
up paintings. Colors can create atmosphere and many artists
think they can be used to express feelings too.

Degas used lots of shades of red in this painting
to give it a warm, homely atmosphere.

If you look at this little boy's hat
up close, you'll see that Seurat added
contrasting blue and orange dots to make
it look brighter. From farther back,
all the colors blend together.

Combing the Hair
About 1896
Hilaire-Germain-Edgar Degas

Bathers at Asnieres
1884
Georges Seurat

Van Gogh painted this vase of sunflowers in the
south of France. He lived near fields full of bright
sunflowers, and he loved walking through them.
For him, the color yellow was a symbol
of happiness and friendship.

Sunflowers
1888
Vincent van Gogh

In this painting, Renoir uses blue and orange, which are 'complementary colors' — pairs of colors that look brighter when seen side by side.

Blue and orange, red and green, and purple and yellow are all complementary colors.

The Skiff
1875
Pierre-Auguste Renoir

Gauguin used simple blocks of bright color to make it look as if the sun was beating down on this harvest scene. He painted the dog red, so that it would really stand out against the green field.

Harvest: Le Pouldu
1890
Paul Gauguin

This pastel drawing shows Ophelia, a character from Shakespeare's play *Hamlet*. Ophelia drowned in a river, surrounded by flowers. But Redon paints her in a strange, imaginary world. He uses rich, blurry colors to make the painting look like a vivid dream.

Ophelia among the Flowers
About 1905-8
Odilon Redon

Bacchus and Ariadne
1520-3
Titian

Perhaps the most striking color in this painting is the bright blue of the sky. At the time, this blue paint was very expensive, because it was made by grinding lapis lazuli, a semi-precious stone.

HIDDEN MEANINGS

There's often more to a painting than meets the eye.
Artists sometimes include objects, animals and places with
extra meanings, to help viewers work out what's really going on.

Pictures of saints often include a symbol, so that people know who they are. Saint Catherine's symbol is a wheel, which she's leaning on here. She was condemned to die on the wheel, but it was broken by a thunderbolt.

Spinning fireworks called Catherine Wheels are named after her.

Saint Catherine of Alexandria
About 1507
Raphael

Portrait of a Woman of the Hofer Family
About 1470
Swabian

This woman is holding a forget-me-not flower so people will remember her. There's also a fly on her headdress that shows off the artist's skills. It almost looks as if a real fly has landed on the painting.

The three saints standing on the left can all be identified by their symbols: an arrow for Saint Edmund, a ring for Saint Edward the Confessor and a lamb for Saint John the Baptist.

The Wilton Diptych
About 1395–9

This painting was probably made for King Richard II. He is shown kneeling on the left. He is wearing a badge of his personal symbol, a white stag. The angels are wearing stag badges too, to show they support him.

On the back of the painting there's a white stag with a crown around its neck.

16

These two men are surrounded by symbols of learning: globes, sundials, books and instruments. But on the floor in front of them lies a strange shape. If you look at it from the correct angle, you can see it's a distorted skull — a symbol of death.

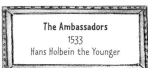

The Ambassadors
1533
Hans Holbein the Younger

If you look closely at the mirror, you can see two people entering the room. One of them is probably the artist himself — who signed his name on the wall above.

This painting of a married couple is packed with symbols. The little dog stands for faithfulness, and the brass chandelier and expensive red hangings show how rich the couple is.

The Arnolfini Portrait
1434
Jan van Eyck

The painting is full of tiny details, like these red shoes.

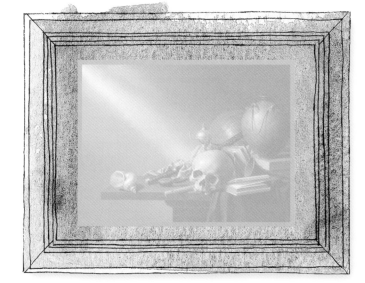

The objects in this still life all have hidden meanings. The books symbolize knowledge, the pipe stands for pleasure, and a rare seashell represents wealth. But in the middle of them is a human skull, to remind us that these things don't last.

An Allegory of the Vanities of Human Life
About 1640
Harmen Steenwyck

FLATTERING PORTRAITS

In the past, rich people paid artists to paint flattering portraits of them. Some artists were very successful and made lots of money, but others didn't always get it right.

Van Dyck painted King Charles I on horseback to make him look impressive. King Charles was actually a very short man - only 5ft (1.5 meters) tall. But the painting is huge, so the King seems to tower over the viewer.

Equestrian Portrait of Charles I
About 1637-8
Anthony van Dyck

Shown here at her embroidery frame, Madame de Pompadour was one of the most important people in 18th-century France. She was only 43 when this was painted — her gray hair is actually a stylish wig.

She was very sick at the time, and died before the painting was finished, but the artist makes her look beautiful and cultured, as she would want to be remembered, with her beloved pet dog beside her.

Madame de Pompadour at her Tambour Frame
1763-4
François-Hubert Drouais

Velázquez was King Philip IV's official painter. The portrait on the left shows Philip in his finest clothes. It was his favorite portrait of himself.

About 20 years later, Velázquez painted the portrait on the right. This time Philip wasn't too happy about looking old, and Velázquez never painted him again.

Philip IV of Spain in Brown and Silver
About 1631–2
Diego Velázquez

Philip IV of Spain
About 1656
Diego Velázquez

Up close, you can see the splotches of paint in Philip's outfit, but from a distance it looks just like an expensive brocade.

King Henry VIII sent Holbein around Europe to paint noble women, so he could choose a bride. Christina wasn't a great beauty, but Holbein makes her delicate hands stand out against her black clothes. When Henry saw this, he said he was in love with her.

But Christina refused to marry him. She knew that Henry had chopped a previous wife's head off. "If I had two heads, one should be at the King of England's disposal," she said.

Christina of Denmark, Duchess of Milan
1538
Hans Holbein the Younger

Queen Charlotte
1789
Sir Thomas Lawrence

When this portrait was finished, Queen Charlotte decided it wasn't flattering enough, so she let the painter keep it.

The Queen looks tired and care-worn, perhaps because her husband, King George III, had just suffered a bout of madness. He once had a chat with a tree that he thought was the King of Prussia.

MAKING A MOCKERY

Some artists painted people to show their bad points.
These paintings are often funny, but they also have a moral.
They make fun of people who are vain, greedy or cruel.

The artist made these tax gatherers look evil and ugly, to show how ugly their greed has made them on the inside.

Two Tax Gatherers
About 1540
Marinus van Reymerswaele

Christ Mocked
About 1490-1500
Hieronymus Bosch

This wrinkly old lady is all dressed up, but her clothes don't suit her at all. The artist was making fun of vain old women who dress in clothes designed for young, beautiful ladies.

She is clutching a rose, which is withering – just like her.

An Old Woman
About 1513
Quinten Massys

In this painting, Jesus is surrounded by four torturers. He looks calm and noble, but his torturers have cruel, horrible faces. The man in the top right-hand corner is wearing a spiky animal collar. This is because the men who tortured Jesus were known in the Bible as "savage beasts."

This is the first in a series of six paintings making fun of the foolish reasons why some people get married. Each of the paintings tells part of the story of a young man and woman who are forced to get married by their families, for money and social standing.

The bride is in tears.

The young man is ignoring his unhappy bride. The dogs chained together in the corner are a symbol of how miserable the young couple will be.

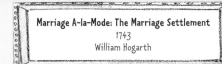

Marriage A-la-Mode: The Marriage Settlement
1743
William Hogarth

Marriage A-la-Mode: The Toilette
1745
William Hogarth

This painting comes later in the same series. The young woman is now married, but her husband is nowhere to be seen. Instead she's surrounded by people who want her money.

This man's expression makes him seem greedy and full of himself.

This vain man has curling papers in his hair.

A Man and a Woman in a Stableyard
Probably 1630
Pieter Quast

The artist has made this soldier look silly and vain. He's showing off his huge floppy hat and his nice new boots, which won't be much use to him in battle.

SELF PORTRAITS

Self portraits allowed artists to try out
new skills without worrying about what anyone else thought.
They also show us how the artists saw themselves.

Self Portrait
About 1880–1
Paul Cézanne

Cézanne, on the left, painted people
just as if they were still lifes. He said it
didn't matter if he was painting "an apple
or a head" as he was only interested in
colors and shapes.

Van Eyck, on the right, was famous
for paintings with amazing attention
to detail and very realistic light
effects, such as this one.

Portrait of a Man (Self Portrait)
1433
Jan van Eyck

This self portrait
advertises Vigée
Le Brun's artistic
skills. She's dressed
up as a fine lady
to show how well
she can paint
fancy clothes —
although it would
have been tricky
to paint in them.

Self Portrait in a Straw Hat
After 1782
Elizabeth Vigée Le Brun

Self Portrait
Probably 1670–3
Bartolomé Esteban Murillo

Murillo painted
this so that his
children would
have something
to remember
him by after his
death — and he
added something
surprising...

...his hand
is reaching out
of the painted
frame.

This is the only known portrait which Gainsborough painted of himself and his family. He often painted people in a natural landscape, which was the fashion at the time.

It might not look like it at first, but Van Gogh's chair is a kind of self portrait. He saw himself as an ordinary working man, so the chair is simple, and it's painted in yellow, his favorite color. Van Gogh also painted an elegant chair with a candle on it as a portrait of his friend, Gauguin.

The Artist with his Wife and Daughter
About 1748
Thomas Gainsborough

Van Gogh signed the picture on the box behind the chair.

Van Gogh's Chair
About 1888
Vincent van Gogh

A Man with a Quilted Sleeve
About 1510
Titian

We don't know who the man in this picture is, but some experts think he could be the artist. Titian could be sitting at his easel and turning his head to look at himself in a mirror.

Rembrandt painted the self portrait on the left at the height of his career. He based it on Titian's 'A Man with a Quilted Sleeve,' above. He's hinting that he's a great painter, just as Titian was.

Self Portrait at the Age of 34
1640
Rembrandt van Rijn

Rembrandt painted the self portrait on the right in the last year of his life. He doesn't seem so vain in his old age. He is wearing plain clothes, and his pose is much less formal.

Self Portrait at the Age of 63
1669
Rembrandt van Rijn

OUT AND ABOUT

Some artists want to capture the hustle and bustle of everyday life. They often paint outside, creating colorful pictures of cafés, circuses, parks and beaches.

Monet painted this picture of his wife and her friend at the seaside. Experts can tell it was painted on the beach because grains of sand got mixed in with the paint.

The Beach at Trouville
1870
Claude-Oscar Monet

Degas used sketchy brushstrokes to paint these ballet dancers doing their exercises.

Miss La La at the Cirque Fernando
1879
Hilaire-Germain-Edgar Degas

Degas shows a famous acrobat, Miss La La, dangling from the ceiling of the circus by gripping a rope between her teeth. The steep angle makes us feel as if we're watching her from the audience below.

Ballet Dancers
About 1890-1900
Edgar Degas

This painting of a busy café looks like a snapshot. You can just see the dancer on stage in the background.

Music in the Tuileries Gardens
1862
Edouard Manet

Corner of a Café-Concert
Probably 1878–80
Edouard Manet

A fashionable crowd is listening to a concert in the Tuileries Gardens in Paris. Manet put himself and his friends in this picture. He's the man right at the edge of the painting.

This is Manet.

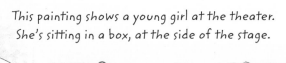

This painting shows a young girl at the theater. She's sitting in a box, at the side of the stage.

Berthe Morisot painted the background of this picture in her local park, but the models posed for her in an indoor studio.

It might seem strange that Renoir left out the stage, but people at the theater often liked looking at each other and showing off their clothes just as much as they liked watching the play.

At the Theater
1876-7
Pierre-Auguste Renoir

Summer's Day
About 1879
Berthe Morisot

MAKING HISTORY

Sometimes paintings capture a moment in history, but they don't always tell both sides of the story. Artists often use pictures to make a particular point.

Goya painted over this portrait of Wellington twice. Each time the Duke won a new medal, Goya changed his outfit and painted on the new medal, to keep it up to date and to show off his victories.

The Duke of Wellington
1812–14
Francisco de Goya

Dashes of white paint make the medals look as though they're gleaming.

This painting celebrates steam trains — still a recent invention at the time. The train speeding toward us stands out against the light colors of the old road bridge and the peaceful countryside.

Rain, Steam and Speed
1844
J.M.W.Turner

Uccello painted 'The Battle of San Romano' to show how great Florence was. It shows a battle between the armies of Florence (on the left) and Siena. It wasn't a very important battle, but Uccello makes it look like a dramatic fight with hundreds of soldiers.

Uccello didn't paint real horses. He copied a model horse over and over again. That's why all the horses look so similar.

This page boy was painted without a helmet to show off his fine features.

The Battle of San Romano
Probably about 1438–40
Paolo Uccello

This painting originally showed the execution of Maximilian, the Emperor of Mexico, and two of his generals — but the part showing Maximilian and one general is missing.

At the time, people thought the painting was very shocking, because it seemed to criticize the French government, who had made Maximilian emperor.

It wasn't exhibited while Manet was alive, and was cut into pieces after his death. Degas eventually bought the surviving pieces and put them all on one canvas.

The Execution of Maximilian
About 1867–8
Edouard Manet

Lady Jane Grey was just seventeen years old when she was executed. She had been Queen of England for only nine days. Delaroche makes her look pure and innocent in her glowing white dress. When this painting was first shown in Paris, some people were so touched by it they wept.

The Execution of Lady Jane Grey
1833
Paul Delaroche

When Colonel Tarleton came back from fighting in the American War of Independence, he asked Reynolds to paint this portrait of him. Many people think he wasn't a very good soldier, but Reynolds makes him look dashing and heroic, with the battle in full swing in the background.

Tarleton lost two fingers from his right hand during the war, which is why his hands are partly hidden.

Colonel Tarleton
1782
Sir Joshua Reynolds

MYTHS AND LEGENDS

Paintings of myths and legends were often packed with tiny details that help to tell the story. They were usually painted for wealthy people who wanted to decorate their homes and show off how many books they'd read.

In this painting, the Greek god Apollo is chasing Daphne, a nature spirit. She prayed for rescue and was turned into a tree as he touched her.

Apollo and Daphne
Probably 1470–80
Antonio del Pollaiuolo

Saint George and the Dragon
About 1470
Paolo Uccello

This painting tells the story of Saint George and the dragon. A dragon had been attacking a city and each day it demanded a young maiden to eat. One day, it was the turn of a princess, but George came to the rescue and defeated the dragon. Then the princess tied her belt around its neck and led it back to the city.

The dragon looks terrifying and terrified at the same time.

In this painting, Venus, the goddess of love, is awake, but Mars, the god of war, has fallen asleep. The message of the painting is that love conquers war.

As Mars sleeps, mischievous creatures called satyrs have stolen his helmet and weapons to play with. One is blowing a conch shell into Mars' ear, but he still doesn't wake up.

In myths, satyrs are naughty woodland spirits, half-man and half-goat.

Venus and Mars
About 1485
Botticelli

You can tell the woman is Venus because she's wearing a pearl brooch. She was often shown wearing pearls because, like them, she was born from a shell.

This painting shows a story from a Greek myth. Paris, Prince of Troy, is kidnapping Helen, who is married to the King of the Greeks. This event started a terrible war called the Trojan War.

The Trojans are about to sail off to Troy, taking Helen with them.

Narcissus
About 1490-9
Follower of Leonardo da Vinci

The Abduction of Helen
About 1450-5
Probably by Zanobi Strozzi

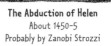

Narcissus fell in love with his own reflection, and died of grief because he could never touch it. His body turned into a Narcissus flower, a kind of small daffodil.

SAINTS AND ANGELS

Many paintings tell stories from the Bible.
The paintings decorated churches and explained the stories
to people who couldn't read them.

In the story of Tobias and the angel, an angel tells a young boy how to cure his father's blindness, using a fish. There's a ghostly-looking dog running along next to the angel. It wasn't originally see-through, but the paint has become more transparent over time.

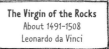

Tobias and the Angel
1470–80
Workshop of Verrocchio

Holy characters such as angels are often shown with halos, circles of light over their heads.

This painting tells two stories from the life of Saint Francis. In the bottom left corner, Francis is giving his cloak to a poor man.

On the right, Francis is shown again, this time lying in bed. When an angel visits him, he has a dream about building a beautiful new church. The church is shown flying in the sky.

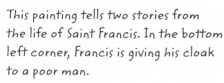

Saint Francis and the Poor Knight, and Francis's Vision
1437–44
Sassetta

The Virgin of the Rocks
About 1491–1508
Leonardo da Vinci

Leonardo painted the Virgin Mary with Jesus, John the Baptist and an angel, against a dark, rocky landscape. At the bottom left-hand corner of the painting there's a clump of Star-of-Bethlehem flowers, which are a symbol of purity.

Tiny, delicate brush strokes make the angel's eyes and mouth look soft and beautiful.

This painting shows Mary and Jesus, surrounded by stories from the lives of different saints. The stickers show Saint Nicholas saving three innocent men from having their heads chopped off, and Saint Margaret being swallowed by a dragon, but escaping unhurt.

The Virgin and Child Enthroned
1260s
Margarito of Arezzo

The Madonna of the Pinks
About 1506–7
Raphael

This picture shows Mary with the baby Jesus. Although they are holy, Raphael painted the scene almost as if they were an ordinary mother and child.

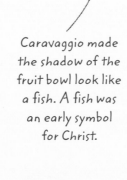

Saint Michael triumphs over the Devil
1468
Bartolomé Bermejo

After Jesus died, two of his followers met a stranger and invited him for dinner. In the middle of the meal they suddenly realized he was Jesus, risen from the dead. Their dramatic gestures show their surprise.

Caravaggio made the shadow of the fruit bowl look like a fish. A fish was an early symbol for Christ.

The Supper at Emmaus
1601
Caravaggio

This is a painting of Saint Michael attacking the devil. The devil is made up of lots of different animals. It has birds' feet, a lizard's tail, and the wings of a moth. The man kneeling on the left paid Bermejo to paint this picture to show how religious he was.

All the paintings in this book are from
the collection of the National Gallery, London.
You can find out more about the gallery and its paintings
by going to the **Usborne Quicklinks Website**
at **www.usborne-quicklinks.com**
and typing in the keywords "art sticker book".

The recommended websites are regularly reviewed and updated but,
please note, Usborne Publishing is not responsible for the content of
any website other than its own. We recommend that young
children are supervised while on the internet.

ACKNOWLEDGEMENTS

Digital images © The Trustees of the National Gallery, London.
(Harvest: Le Pouldu on long term loan from Tate.)

Additional illustrations by Abigail Brown and Nathalie Oger

Digital manipulation by John Russell

First published in 2009 by Usborne Publishing Ltd.,
Usborne House, 83-85 Saffron Hill, London EC1N 8RT, England. www.usborne.com
First published in America in 2009. AE. Copyright © 2009 Usborne Publishing Ltd.

CHILDREN

pages 6-7

More FABULOUS FASHION stickers...

NATURE

pages 8–9

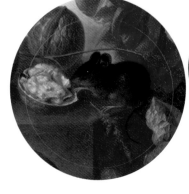

LIGHT

pages 12–13

More LIGHT stickers...

COLOR

pages 14–15

FLATTERING PORTRAITS

pages 18–19

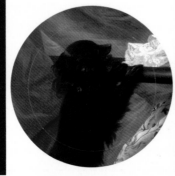

More FLATTERING PORTRAITS stickers...

Making a Mockery

pages 22–23

Self Portraits

pages 24–25

OUT AND ABOUT

pages 26–27

More SELF PORTRAITS stickers...

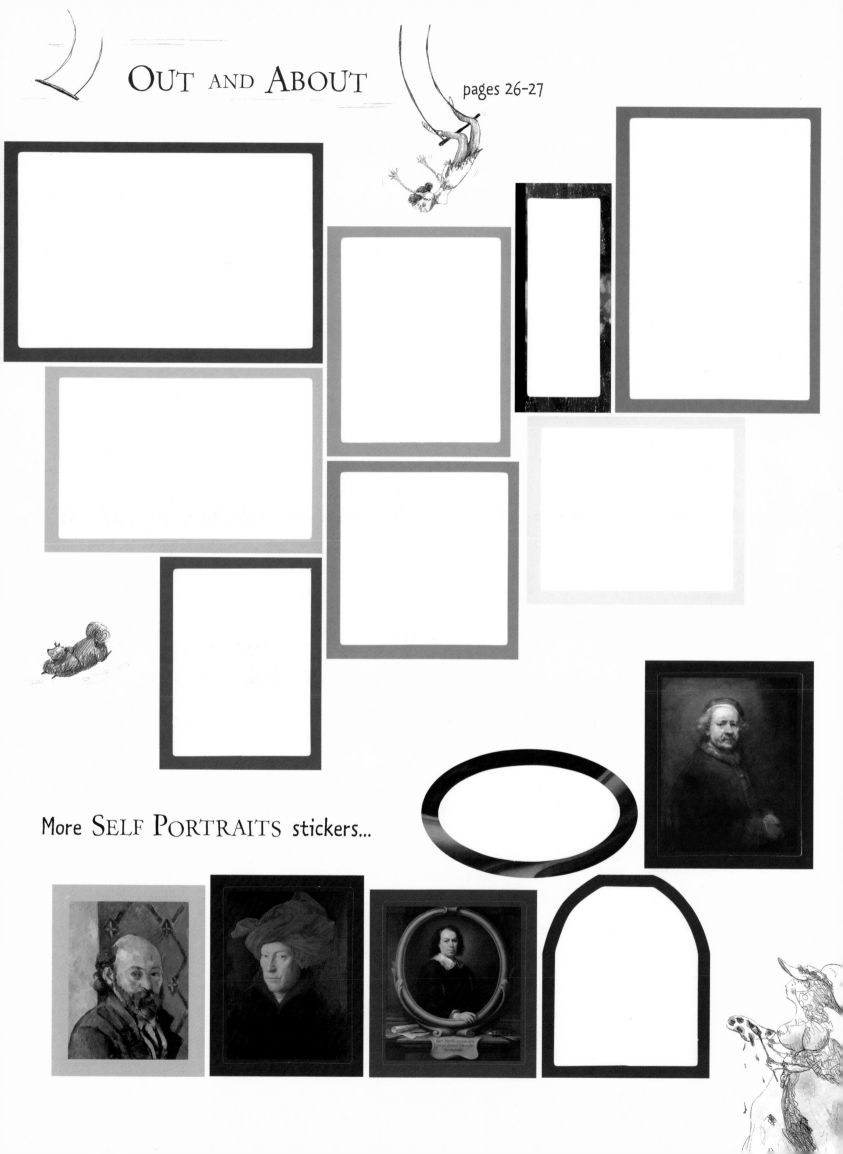

MAKING HISTORY

pages 26–27

MYTHS AND LEGENDS

pages 28–29

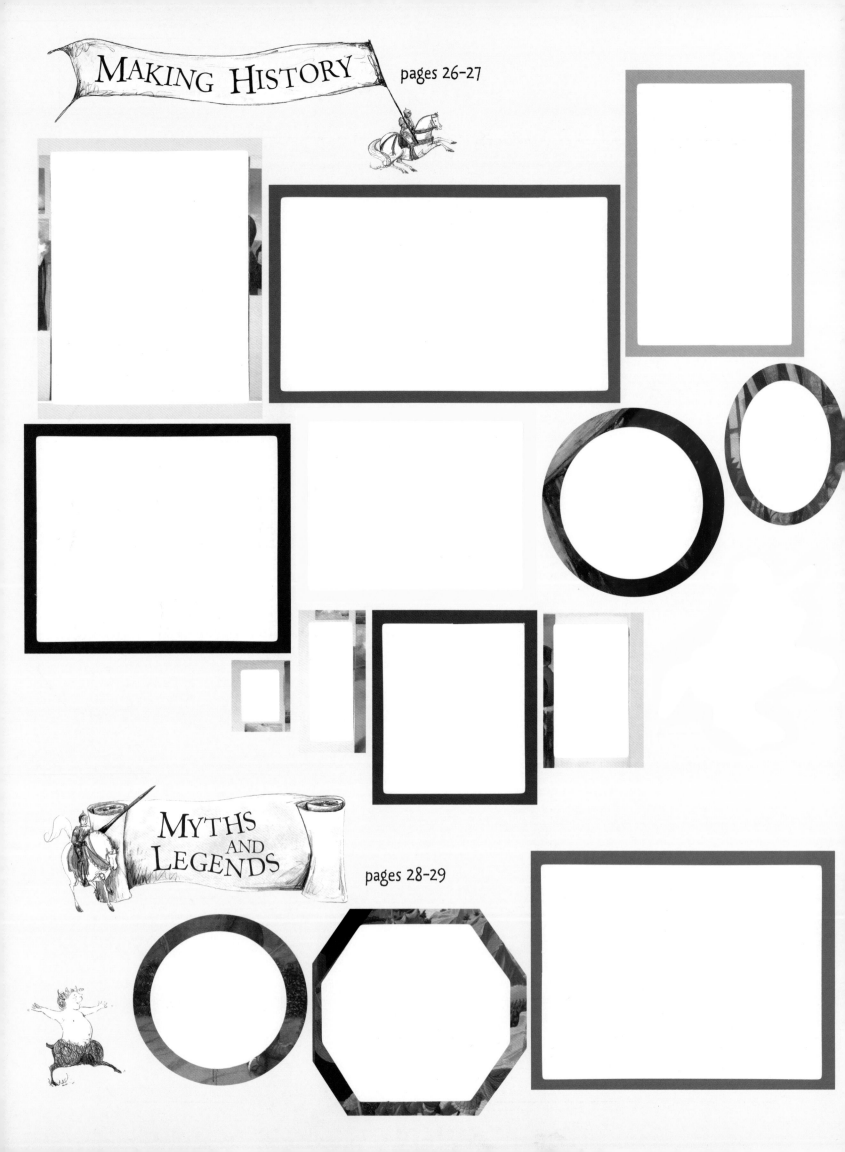

SAINTS AND ANGELS

pages 30-31

More MYTHS AND LEGENDS stickers...

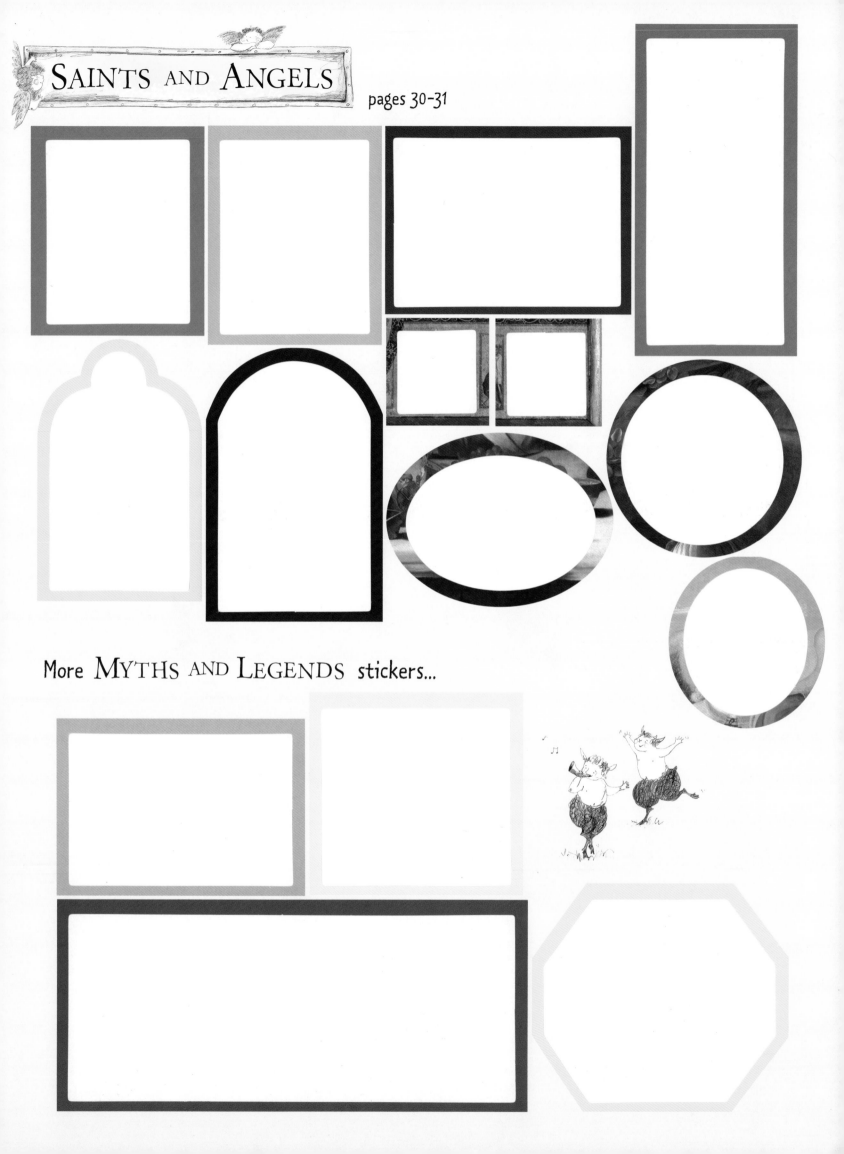